TEEN PREGNANCY
AND WHAT
COMES NEXT

WOMEN
IN THE
WORLD™

TEEN PREGNANCY AND WHAT COMES NEXT

LENA KOYA AND MARY-LANE KAMBERG

Rosen
YA™
New York

Published in 2018 by The Rosen Publishing Group, Inc.
29 East 21st Street, New York, NY 10010

Copyright © 2018 by The Rosen Publishing Group, Inc.

First Edition

Library of Congress Cataloging-in-Publication Data

Names: Koya, Lena, author. | Kamberg, Mary-Lane, author.
Title: Teen pregnancy and what comes next / Lena Koya and Mary-Lane Kamberg.
Description: New York: Rosen Publishing, 2018 | Series: Women in the world |
Audience: Grades 7–12. | Includes bibliographical references and index.
Identifiers: ISBN 9781508177227 (library bound) | ISBN 9781508178583 (paperback)
Subjects: LCSH: Teenage pregnancy—Juvenile literature. | Teenage mothers—Juvenile literature. | Teenagers--Sexual behavior—Juvenile literature.
Classification: LCC HQ759.4 K69 2018 | DDC 306.874'3—dc23

Manufactured in China

CONTENTS

inding out that you are pregnant or that your partner is expecting a baby is a life-changing moment. But it can be scary if this happy event is unplanned and unexpected. And it can be particularly scary as a teenager, when you have perhaps not yet finished school and haven't yet begun your career. According to the US Department of Health and Human Services, approximately 77 percent of all teen births are unplanned. In 2015, according to World Bank data, there were twenty-one births for every one thousand women in the United States aged from fifteen to nineteen years old. In Canada, there were nine births for every one thousand adolescent women. In fact, the teen birth rate in the United States is higher than in many other countries, including Canada and the United Kingdom.

Researchers believe that one reason for this is because American teens are less likely to

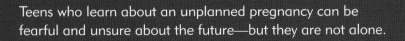
Teens who learn about an unplanned pregnancy can be fearful and unsure about the future—but they are not alone.

use contraception than their counterparts in Canada and Europe. They are more likely to have only limited access to health care. According to the Guttmacher Institute, increased contraception use led to a 25 percent decline in teen pregnancy in the United States between 2007 and 2011. Access to contraception and reproductive health care is an important right all teens should be aware of, whether or not they have dealt with an unplanned pregnancy.

While these statistics might not matter too much if you or your partner is pregnant, it is important to know that there are many others out there in your situation. It is also important to know about the role of contraception in preventing future unplanned pregnancies. But, in the moment of discovering an unplanned pregnancy, many teens are faced with a seemingly overwhelming amount of choices. Will they have the baby or instead opt for an abortion? Will they raise the baby or choose adoption or foster care instead? There is no wrong answer and teens should choose what feels right and comfortable for them. The most important thing is to research all of the available options and to talk about it with a support system, whether that is a partner, family, friends, or medical professionals.

Keeping a baby is a lifelong responsibility. It takes dedication, time, and patience, as well as money and lots of support. Teens who choose to keep their babies face many obstacles that older parents might not, including social stigma, poverty, school absences, and work conflicts. However, with dedication, patience, and support, they can become good parents and live happy lives with their children.

The first step is learning about what to expect before and after the birth. It is important to pick a health care professional and learn about how to keep yourself and your child healthy during pregnancy and after birth. Expectant parents will also need to plan ahead for childcare, the medical needs of an infant, and housing arrangements. Arm yourself with as much information as you can gather. This will help you make strong, informed decisions for both you and your child.

Parenting is a lifelong adventure that brings with it both highs and lows. With information and support, you can temper the lows and enjoy the highs. Welcome to parenthood.

CHAPTER 1

THE FIRST STEPS

For teens under the age of nineteen, nearly four out of five pregnancies are unplanned. Among the general adult population, nearly 50 percent of all pregnancies are not expected or planned. This is largely because of the fact that teens are likely to be more fertile than adults and have less access to contraception. They are also less likely to use contraception properly.

However, thanks largely to increased education about teen pregnancy and increased contraceptive use, the teen birth rate in the United States has fallen to historic lows. For the first time since the US government has begun collecting data, the birth rate has fallen below twenty-five births per thousand teen females, according to the Centers for Disease Control (CDC). Similar decreases appear throughout

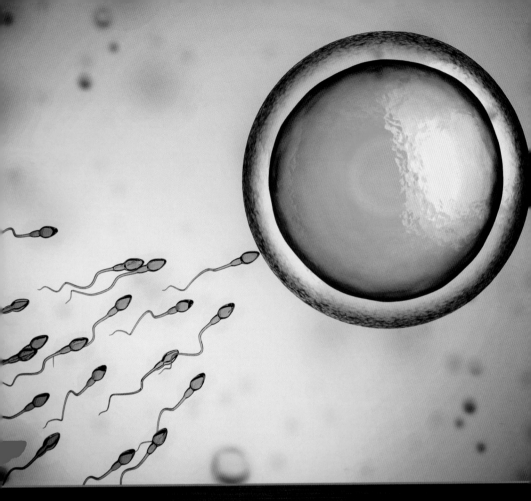

Conception occurs when a sperm successfully penetrates and fertilizes an egg. The fertilized egg will become known as a zygote.

the industrialized world. Indeed, researchers state that education about the proper use of contraception, as well as greater access to birth control, might be the largest factor in this historic decrease.

For teens who choose to responsibly engage in sexual activity, it is essential to read and follow the instructions provided with each form of contraception and to use multiple forms when sexually active, such as using both oral contraceptives and condoms. Different forms of contraception also have different rates of success at preventing pregnancy. Within two years of using the withdrawal method, for example, 43 percent of young women will become pregnant. This percentage dips to 27.5 percent for those who use condoms, 14 percent for those who use oral contraceptives, and 8.5 percent for those who use intrauterine devices (IUDs). Of course, the lowest pregnancy rate (zero) comes from complete abstinence. The highest comes from unprotected sex.

FERTILIZATION

Conception usually occurs within twenty-four hours of ovulation, the time the ovary releases a mature egg. Fertilization occurs when a sperm penetrates the egg.

The fertilized egg is called a zygote. Within the first twenty-four hours, cells begin to divide. The developing baby is called an embryo until the eighth week of growth. After that, it is called a fetus.

Beginning at conception the mother's body produces a hormone called human chorionic gonadotropin (HCG). HCG is a pregnancy hormone present in the blood. About three days after conception, the embryo attaches to the lining of the uterus and continues to grow. The uterus is a hollow, pear-shaped organ in a woman's lower abdomen. Some women experience slight bleeding called spotting for a day or two when implantation occurs.

Some mothers say they "knew" the exact moment they became pregnant. Others identify certain symptoms within one week of conception. Still others don't suspect pregnancy or notice any symptoms for four or more weeks. Every woman's experience is different. And every pregnancy is different, even for the same woman.

EARLY SIGNS

Early signs of pregnancy include a missed menstrual period (or only a brief, light period), tender or swollen breasts, nausea or vomiting ("morning sickness"), fatigue, frequent urination, and mood swings. If you have missed a period and have any or many of these symptoms, you may want to take a home pregnancy test. These are available at any pharmacy. They can be quite reliable even early in a pregnancy. However, it may take two or three weeks after fertilization for the hormone to occur in high enough amounts to be detected.

Home pregnancy tests look for the presence of HCG in the urine. The hormone is only present if you're pregnant or if you have recently given birth or had a miscarriage. Home tests are about 97 percent accurate,

Persistent nausea and vomiting—commonly called
morning sickness—can be one of the early signs

according to WebMD.com. You can increase the accuracy of the result by checking the expiration date on the package and carefully following the directions. The best time of day to test is the first urination of the day when the urine is more concentrated.

Some medications can cause positive results in women who are not pregnant. Avoid aspirin at least twenty-four hours before testing. If you're taking tranquilizers or anticonvulsants, you can also get a false positive result. On the other hand, diuretics or antihistamines may give a negative reading even if you really are pregnant.

If the home test is positive—or if it's negative but you think you really might be pregnant—seek confirmation from a health care provider. You'll get another type of pregnancy test that is typically done in a medical lab, doctor's office, or clinic. It also tests for HCG, but looks for the hormone in the blood. The health care provider will also perform a pelvic exam to confirm the pregnancy and gauge the size of the uterus.

BUILDING A SUPPORT SYSTEM

An unexpected pregnancy can be a challenging experience—particularly if there isn't a support network in place. Young women who are pregnant should not have to keep their pregnancies a secret.

Indeed, a pregnancy cannot be kept a secret for long. It may be difficult to tell parents what is going on, but they will help in the early stages of planning.

Another choice is to speak with a counselor. You can talk to a counselor without parental consent, even if you're younger than eighteen. The counselor will help you make your own decisions based on accurate information about available alternatives. You might also confide in a trusted family member, teacher, or clergyperson. If you want to keep the pregnancy quiet until you've made final decisions, be careful about sharing the news with friends. Gossip spreads fast, especially with the use of social media.

SINGLE MOTHERS

Along with financial help, a young parent needs a support system. This is particularly true for young women, who often face greater social stigma than men.

Often, single teen moms face criticism for their choices. Friends, classmates, or even family members may act differently or pass judgment on a new teenage

HELPING SINGLE TEEN MOTHERS

There are many programs available to help young, single mothers. The Assisting Young Mothers Program (AYM) was developed to help find housing for young women between the ages of sixteen and twenty-four, whether they are pregnant or have young children. The program includes training sessions on parenting, job readiness, and self-sufficiency and take place in independent townhomes. Women are required to work thirty hours per week, but all of their basic living costs are covered in the program. The goal of the program is to teach young mothers self-sufficiency so that they can eventually reach full independence, while continuing to receive community-based support throughout their journey as parents.

mom, leading to isolation. Teen mothers can be at risk for a higher rate of depression, which can result in bad health outcomes for mom and her baby.

Depending on the situation, this support system can include a single mother's immediate and extended family, the father's family, or friends. If teen mothers don't know any other teens with babies, they may be able to connect with other new mothers in childbirth classes or at a daycare provider.

Support can also include services and programs available in the community. One such program is Women, Infants, and Children (WIC). This government program provides nutrition education, supplemental food, and health care referrals to low-income families even before the baby is born. For help with breastfeeding, the La Leche League provides services through a network of mothers who can assist with information and advice.

Young single mothers face the same challenges as parents with partners although, without a partner to aid in parenting, these challenges can become overwhelming. Time is something they never have enough of. A baby requires a lot of care. A single mother is likely to have to juggle childcare with school or a job—or both. And don't forget sleep. New mothers need a lot of it. One

Young infants require lots of care. On top of this, young parents often have to juggle work or school, all while fitting

tip is to rest while the baby naps, especially right at first, regardless of what other work around the house needs to be done.

EDUCATION AND PARENTHOOD

Getting an education or job training is an important way to establish a financially stable environment for your child. Fortunately, many public school systems offer alternative programs that let high school students continue their education in a nontraditional way. Or, a young parent can earn a high school equivalency diploma granted by passing a test called the General Educational Development (GED) test. It is also often referred to as a General Education Diploma. The test is developed by the American Council on Education, the coordinating body for America's higher education institutions. Candidates can take online preparation classes, but the test must be taken in person.

For further education, many universities offer degree programs where students take classes online rather than attending in person. Vocational training for such jobs as bookkeeping, paralegal services, tax preparation, or work in trades like carpentry or plumbing is also available online or in person. The US government operates job training and job placement programs through the Department of Labor, Department of Education, and Department of Health and Human Services. Private enterprises also offer programs that help students acquire skills they need in the workplace.

Even if you must support yourself financially, time constraints may prevent full-time employment—especially if you're still in school. Part-time jobs often pay less per hour than full-time ones, but every bit helps. Look for a job with an understanding boss and flexible hours or one that can be done from home. Some job sites offer childcare to employees, so consider applying for employment at one of them.

Juggling work or school and raising a child is one of the most difficult parts of parenthood. Never be afraid to ask your support system for help (if you need a babysitter for an hour or two during a job interview, for example).

PREPARING FOR CHILDBIRTH

Today, mothers have a wide range of options for the labor and birth of their child. They can decide to give birth in a hospital with an obstetrician or with a midwife, or to give birth in a birthing center with less medical intervention. Some women also choose to have their

Today's young women have many options regarding where and how to give birth. Some might choose to give birth in a hospital setting, while others might choose a birthing center.

babies at home or in birthing tubs. It is important to remember that soon-to-be mothers should choose the most comfortable and safe setting for their particular circumstance and that childbirth does not always go according to plan.

CHILDBIRTH CLASSES

It's perfectly normal to have some fears about childbirth. Childbirth education helps expectant mothers know what to expect once labor begins. Childbirth classes will arm you with information, reassurance, and coping techniques to ease your mind before labor and help you through it when it starts. In some states Medicaid pays for childbirth education for low-income mothers. Or, you may qualify for a reduced fee.

You can choose the type of classes you want. You have many choices, and many of the methods share the same attitudes toward birth as a normal process. Among the most popular methods today include hospital-based classes, Lamaze, the Bradley Method, Birthing from Within, Birth Works, and birth hypnosis. Hospital-based classes often offer instruction in the stages of labor, pain management, potential complications, and medical procedures. Your practitioner can recommend classes, or you can look for them in your community.

Lamaze classes show pregnant women how to use breathing and other strategies to help them get through labor and birth. Its philosophy includes a holistic view of natural, normal childbirth. It encourages waiting for labor to start on its own and letting women eat, drink, and move around during labor. And it empowers women to make informed decisions should medical intervention be desired or necessary.

The Bradley Method focuses on the benefits of drug-free birth, for both the mother and baby. It uses slow, deep breathing and other techniques to help the mother achieve complete relaxation. Classes also include information about nutrition, exercise, bonding, and breastfeeding. The method stresses the importance of a birthing coach who is close to the mother and who is likely to be active in the baby's life.

Birthing from Within is a method that uses information along with spiritual and creative art projects to help mothers-to-be deal with expectations, fears, and other emotions concerning childbirth. Instructors don't promote any particular childbirth method, but they support natural birth if that is what the mother wants.

Several types of birth hypnosis teach women to train themselves to deal with pain without fear or anxiety. Some new mothers give the method rave reviews. Others report it didn't help them at all.

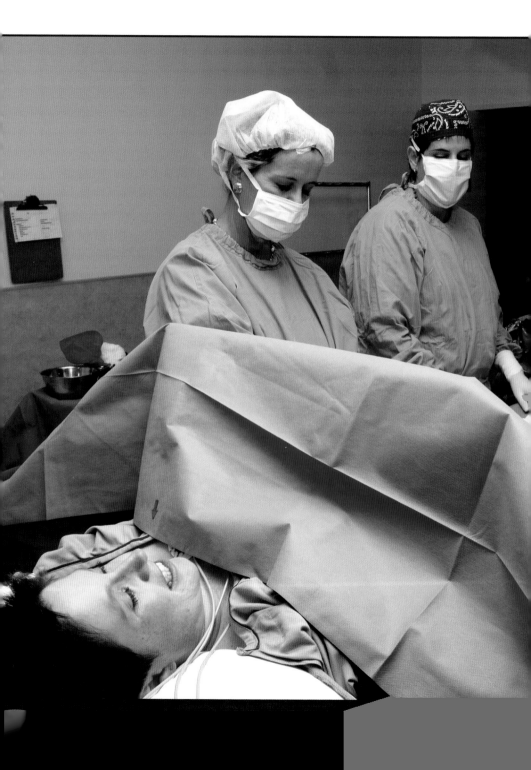

C-SECTIONS

Most women give birth vaginally, but some have a surgical procedure called a cesarean section (C-section). Under a local or general anesthetic, a doctor cuts into the mother's abdomen and lifts the baby out. The surgery has been used since ancient times. But most of the cesarean procedures back then were performed to deliver the baby from mothers who had already died in the birthing process or were dying and could not be helped.

A C-section is major surgery. Many are performed for medical reasons involving the mother or baby's health, and a few are requested by the mother. According to the Centers for Disease Control and Prevention (CDC), over 32 percent of women in the United States have C-sections. In nearly 90 percent of the cases, a physician made the

ELIMINATING DISPARITIES IN TEEN PREGNANCY

According to the Centers for Disease Control (CDC), US teen birth rates dropped 9 percent from 2013 to 2014. However, racial and ethnic disparities continue to exist in US teen pregnancy rates. In 2014, African American and Hispanic teen birth rates were two times higher than for Caucasian teens. The reasons why African American and Hispanic teens are more likely to become pregnant as teenagers are varied and complex. However, differences in socioeconomic opportunities are likely a major reason. Poor teens of color are less likely to have access to high-quality medical care, including access to contraception, than more economically advantaged white teens.

In order to address these disparities, the CDC has implemented a multistep approach: work within communities to decrease inequality; invest in advocacy and educational programs to prevent teen pregnancies; increase access to contraception and high-quality medical care; and educate community leaders, parents, and teens about the connections between social inequalities and teen pregnancy.

decision either before or during labor. The remaining 10 percent of C-sections performed were done at the mother's request. A 2010 *Obstetrics and Gynecology* poll of more than five thousand obstetricians found that 29 percent said they performed more C-sections today than in the past because they feared lawsuits should something go wrong with a vaginal birth. Like all surgeries, C-section deliveries carry risks. These risks should not be taken lightly.

BIRTH PLANS

After investigating ways to deal with labor and birth, as well as whether to give birth in a hospital delivery room, birth center, or home, it's a good idea to develop a written birth plan. A birth plan is a list of your preferences for what happens during and after labor and birth.

A birth plan includes such items as:

- Where will the baby be born?
- Who will assist in the process?
- How do you want to handle pain relief?
- What kind of environment do you want for childbirth?
- What backup plan is in place should you change your mind about pain management or if an emergency arises?

Writing a birth plan—a list of preferences for treatment and the environment you desire during labor and delivery—is an important way to understand and express your expectations for the birth of your child.

- What choice of positions will you want during labor and delivery?
- Do you want soft music playing and/or the lights dimmed for the baby's birth?
- Which newborn tests can be done right away, and which can be delayed or declined?
- Do you want to hold and feed the baby right away?

Discuss your plan with the practitioner who will attend the birth. Remember, these are your preferences. Actual events may differ. Having a birth plan in place doesn't guarantee you'll get everything on your list. Unexpected occurrences may dictate different choices. Or, you might change your mind during the process. However, a birth plan lets your childbirth team work with you while at the same time considering your health and the health of the baby. A birth plan can also help you choose a health care provider and the place you want to have your baby.

CHOOSING A PRACTITIONER

Pregnant women can get labor and delivery care from an obstetrician or a family practice doctor. Doctors may practice in private offices or clinics. They might also get prenatal care from a certified nurse-midwife who practices at a hospital or birth center or a certified professional midwife who practices at a birth center as well as the client's home for home births. All midwives have a connection with a medical doctor they can call on if a problem or emergency occurs. To find a practitioner, ask for referrals from your primary care doctor or friends and family.

Also consider using the services of a doula during labor and birth. A doula is a nonmedical person who provides physical and emotional support during

Young women can choose what kind of provider they would like to have for prenatal care, labor, and delivery. It is important for young women to speak to a provider about their expectations and to feel comfortable with their choice.

pregnancy, labor, birth, and the period after the baby arrives. Doulas often work in conjunction with midwives. The doula's services include such techniques as massage, aromatherapy, visualization, and positioning during labor. The doula also acts as a spokesperson for the mother when communicating preferences with medical staff. Depending on the arrangement with the new mother, the doula may also visit the mother and child at home after the birth or help answer questions about breastfeeding or other baby care.

The choice of where to give birth will depend on a number of factors. What kind of birth plan do you want to create? You may choose a traditional hospital setting. Or, you may prefer an alternative birth center or have your baby at home to avoid medical interventions like fetal monitoring, pain medicine or other drugs, or C-section deliveries that may not be necessary if you and the baby are at low risk for complications.

When deciding on a provider, ask about the professional's philosophy concerning labor and birth. Discuss your choice of hospital, birth center, or home. Other factors include the office location and hours and whether you'll see the same person for all prenatal appointments. Also think about the person's personality and whether you feel comfortable with him or her.

It is also important to line up a birth coach to help during labor. This could be the mother's partner. It could also be a family member. This person should attend childbirth education classes with the mother to learn what his or her role will be.

A HEALTHY PREGNANCY

For pregnant women who decide to carry their babies to term, the first step is to seek prenatal health care. Regular checkups are needed to help stay healthy during pregnancy. Health care providers also order screening tests at various points throughout the pregnancy, although this is at the discretion of the mother. Prenatal care is especially important for teens. Teens often have low birth weight babies, who have a higher risk of serious illness. Teens commonly also have poor diets without many of the nutrients the growing babies need.

Prenatal care gives you the opportunity to get information about nutrition, exercise, labor, and the birthing process. Babies in the womb eat what the mother eats and drink what she drinks. Eating a wide variety of foods and taking a daily

prenatal vitamin will help ensure that both mother and baby get the nutrients they need. Weight gain is extremely important during this time, and not gaining an appropriate amount of weight can result in low birth weight and lead to developmental problems for the baby. Throughout the pregnancy, it is important to follow a healthy diet that is low on sugar and higher in protein, vitamins, and minerals. Especially important are iron, calcium, protein, folic acid, and vitamins A, B^6, B^{12}, and C in the right amounts.

According to Brenda J. Lane and Ilana T. Kirsch, authors of the *Knack Pregnancy Guide*, pregnant women need 3,300 international units (IUs) of vitamin A each day. But too much of the vitamin can harm the growing baby. Be aware that some acne treatments have high levels of this vitamin. Consult a health care provider before taking these or any other medicines while pregnant. Also avoid alcohol, nicotine, and recreational drugs. These can have devastating effects on the developing baby or after he or she is born, if breastfeeding.

Staying hydrated while you're expecting is also important. Recommended drinks include water, skim milk, green tea, and cranberry juice diluted with water or seltzer. Most doctors recommend avoiding drinking too many sugary drinks, including most juices, or too much caffeine.

Expectant mothers also need physical activity for a healthy pregnancy. Along with being good for the baby, exercise reduces some of the discomfort pregnant women often experience. It reduces the risk of preterm labor, increases stamina for the labor and birth, and contributes to recovery afterward. Always check with a care provider before embarking on an exercise plan.

Some activities should be avoided, especially horseback riding, downhill skiing, scuba diving, gymnastics, and contact sports like basketball. Some good choices—especially in early pregnancy—are low-impact exercise like walking, swimming, and water aerobics (but avoid hot tubs). Or join a prenatal exercise class led by a reputable organization.

CALCULATING THE DUE DATE

One of the first items on the prenatal agenda is figuring out the baby's due date. To estimate the date, use the first day of the mother's most recent period as the starting point. Then count forty weeks ahead. A due date is only an educated guess based on average human gestation, the time a baby grows in the uterus. If unsure of the last menstrual cycle, an ultrasound between the eighth and eighteenth weeks of pregnancy can be used to determine when to expect birth.

THE FIRST TRIMESTER

The forty weeks of pregnancy are grouped into three stages of three months each called trimesters. Each trimester is characterized by different signs and

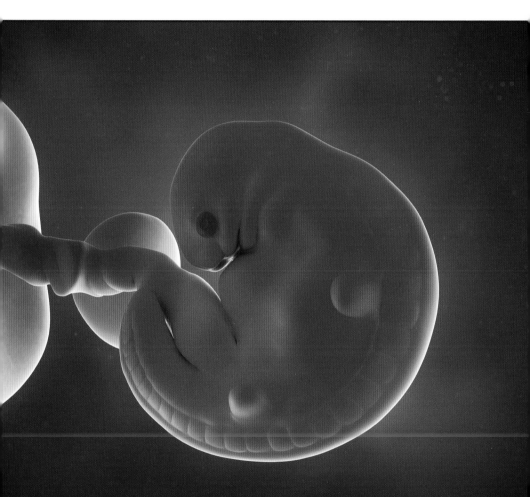

During the first eight weeks of pregnancy, the baby is called an embryo. The external features that will make it look more like a human baby develop toward the end of this stage.

39

developments in the mother and child. The first twelve weeks mark hormonal changes in the mother. These changes affect most organ systems. In addition to early symptoms of pregnancy, pregnant women may experience food cravings or distaste for certain foods, constipation, headache, heartburn, and weight gain. In early pregnancy they might even lose weight. Pregnant women may experience all of these symptoms or some or none of them.

During the first trimester the baby, called an embryo, is busy forming the heart, brain, and spinal cord. Little stumps that will become arms and legs appear. At eight weeks, the baby has a regular heartbeat. Major body structures and organs—including sex organs—have begun to form. Arms and legs lengthen, and fingers and toes start to develop. The eyes, which now have eyelids, move from the side to the front of the face. The baby is about 1 inch (2.5 centimeters) long and weighs 0.12 ounces (3 grams). From the end of eight weeks to birth, the baby is called a fetus.

Over the next four weeks the fetus will grow to about 3 inches (8 cm) long and weigh close to 1 ounce (28 g). Nerves and muscles work together well enough for the fetus to make a fist. External sex organs have formed. The eyelids close and will not open until the end of the second trimester. This protects developing eyes.

THE SECOND TRIMESTER

By the thirteenth week of pregnancy, tiredness and nausea typically ease. The abdomen expands to make room for the growing fetus. Pregnant women may

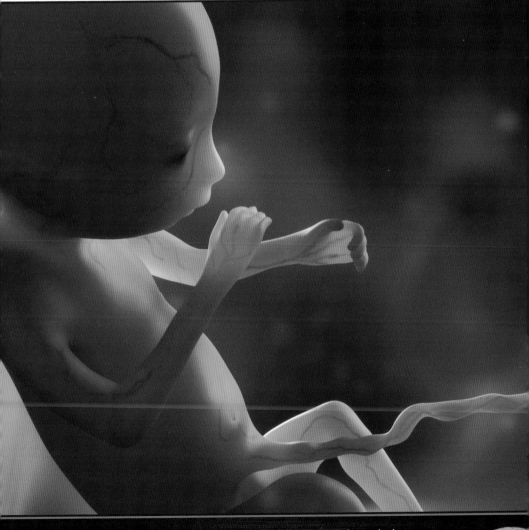

At sixteen weeks, a fetus grows a more complete skeleton.

experience aches and pains in the back, abdomen, groin, or thighs. Skin around the nipples may darken. Stretch marks can develop on the abdomen, breast, thighs, or buttocks, as well as a line on the skin between the pubic hairline and navel, which is called a linea nigra.

The hands may feel numb or tingle. In some women hormonal changes cause fluid retention and increase the risk of carpal tunnel syndrome. Symptoms usually disappear after childbirth. Some women also experience itching on the abdomen, hands, or feet or swelling of the face, fingers, or ankles. Call a health care provider if the itching is accompanied by fatigue, nausea, loss of appetite, or yellowish skin or eyes. This can indicate liver trouble. Also call a provider for sudden or excessive swelling or rapid weight gain. These symptoms can indicate a complication of the pregnancy.

At sixteen weeks, the fetus is getting a more complete skeleton as bone continues to grow. Skin begins to form. The fetus exhibits the sucking reflex. He or she is between 4 and 5 inches long (10–13 cm) and weighs about 3 ounces (85 g). By twenty weeks—halfway through the gestation period—pregnant women may feel a slight fluttering that some describe as butterflies. At first the sensation is so slight it feels like gas. As the baby grows and becomes more active, the movement becomes more noticeable. At this point the baby can hear and swallow. She or he has eyebrows, eyelashes, fingernails, and toenails. The length is about 6 inches (15 cm), and the weight has increased to about 9 ounces (255 g).

Between twenty-four and twenty-eight weeks the baby is fine-tuning. Taste buds, footprints, and fingerprints form. Hair grows on the head. Sex organs are developed and in place. The baby regularly sleeps and wakes. He or she has grown to about 12 inches (30 cm) long and weighs about 1.5 pounds (680 g).

THIRD TRIMESTER

By the beginning of the third trimester at twenty-nine weeks, the growing baby presses against the mother's organs. Pregnant women may experience some of the same signs of the second trimester along with shortness of breath, heartburn, leaky breasts, or hemorrhoids. They may have trouble sleeping or notice contractions that may or may not lead to labor. Contractions are the periodic tightening and relaxing of the uterus.

During this time, the cervix thins and softens, which helps open the birth canal. The baby will kick or punch forcefully, leaving no doubt that he or she is there. By the thirty-second week, the fetus has a complete but soft skeleton. The eyes open and close. The lungs are still developing. The baby gains weight faster than before—about 0.5 pounds (227 g) per week. At thirty-six weeks the baby weighs about 6

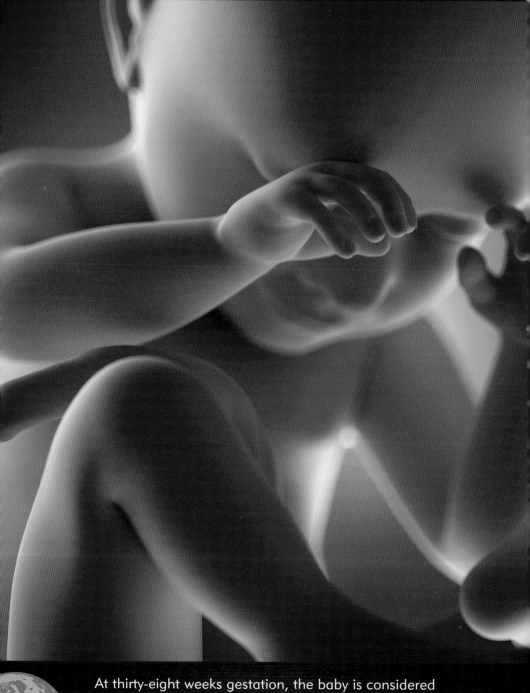

At thirty-eight weeks gestation, the baby is considered full term.

pounds (3 kilograms) and "stands" between 16 and 19 inches (41–48 cm) tall. At thirty-eight weeks, the baby is considered full term. The organs can function on their own. Now the baby is ready to live outside the mother's body.

COMMON COMPLICATIONS

Health problems for the mother or baby during pregnancy are known as complications of pregnancy. If a woman already had health problems before pregnancy, they can have effects during it. Other complications in mothers-to-be arise during pregnancy. Many disappear after delivery. Fortunately, most of them can be managed during the pregnancy with proper health care. These may include such conditions as:

- Anemia, a low number of red blood cells that causes weakness, fatigue, pale skin, or shortness of breath.
- Depression, feelings of extreme

sadness during or after pregnancy.
- Ectopic pregnancy, a fertilized egg that implants outside the uterus, typically in the fallopian tubes that connect the ovaries to the uterus.
- Gestational diabetes, or high blood sugar.
- Severe, persistent nausea or vomiting.
- Preeclampsia (also known as toxemia), a condition marked by high blood pressure, swelling of hands and face, stomach pain, and headaches.
- Fetal problems like poor growth or heart trouble are also considered pregnancy complications.

MYTHS AND
FACTS

There are many myths that circulate about pregnancy and birth. Here are three of the most common:

MYTH: Pregnant women should eat enough calories for two.

FACT: Babies actually require fewer extra calories than is commonly believed. During the first trimester, a woman should not add any extra calories to her diet. In the second trimester, she will need approximately 350 more calories each day. By the third trimester, she will need to take in approximately 450 extra calories for the growing baby's needs.

MYTH: You cannot get pregnant while breastfeeding.

FACT: While women often do not ovulate while exclusively breastfeeding, some women can still get pregnant. When the baby eats food in addition to nursing, it is more likely for a woman to get pregnant even while breastfeeding.

MYTH: You shouldn't drink caffeine while pregnant.

FACT: There is no evidence that moderate caffeine use during pregnancy harms the baby. Contrary to popular opinion, it is also beneficial to eat fish during pregnancy, as long as the fish is cooked and you eat it in moderation.

CHAPTER 4

GETTING READY FOR PARENTHOOD

While mothers may be able to fit in regular clothes for most (if not all) of the first trimester, by the second trimester their clothes will be getting tight as their belly grows to fit the baby. Maternity clothes are designed with the comfort of the mother-to-be in mind and can be used throughout pregnancy. They are typically designed with loose or elastic materials so that they can expand with the growing baby. Remember that pregnant women only need six to seven months of maternity clothes, so don't buy too much. Many mothers-to-be can even buy gently used maternity clothes or get hand-me-downs from friends or family members.

Babies have few needs outside of sleeping, eating, staying dry and warm, and getting love and affection. A lot of baby equipment is not necessary, except for a car seat, a place to sleep, and a carrier or stroller.

BABY EQUIPMENT

Stores that cater to new parents have plenty of items in stock. However, you won't need one of each. You won't need many of the available baby goods at all. A newborn's needs are simple. She or he needs to eat, stay dry and warm, and have a place to sleep. First shop for things you would need on hand if the baby arrived "today."

If planning to breastfeed, there is no need for bottle systems. However, if the mother plans to return to school or work and someone else will be babysitting, look into buying a breast pump to express and store breast milk in bottles the caregiver can use. Get just a few bottles to get started. You can get more later.

Keeping baby dry is easily solved with a supply of cloth or disposable diapers. These come in different sizes to fit preemies up through about two years of age. Buy only a package or two of the newborn size until you see how big the baby is. Remember that babies grow fast. You don't want a huge supply of diapers that are too small to use. You'll also need a diaper pail for dirty diapers, a diaper bag for quick trips, and some burp cloths to use when feeding the infant.

Keeping baby warm means clothes and blankets. Depending on the season, look for T-shirts or "onesies," short- or long-sleeved bodysuits with bottom snaps that easily tuck into pants or shorts. One-piece sleepers or sleep sacks are great, especially for the first several weeks. Sleep sacks are similar to sleeping bags used for camping, except the top part has sleeves. It's like a blanket with a built-in sleeper.

Newborns often need hats and socks to keep warm. (To wash baby socks, put them in a mesh bag together before throwing them in a washing machine. They'll be easier to match when they come out.) You'll also need some soft, lightweight blankets called receiving blankets.

Babies should be kept warm in sleep sacks or thick sleepers while sleeping and should never be left alone to sleep with loose blankets.

SLEEP SOLUTIONS

A place for the baby to sleep depends in part on your parenting philosophy. When the baby is first born, he or she will need to be fed every couple of hours. Some parents want to put the baby to sleep in a crib in a separate room. Or, for ease in getting to the baby in the middle of the night, some parents use a bassinet or cradle in their own room.

Some mothers choose to bring their babies to bed with them. Cosleeping makes breastfeeding easier during the night. It also contributes to the mother-child bond and helps the infant sleep better. But there are some risks. A baby should never sleep with the mother on a sofa, water bed, or very soft mattress. Other dangers include mothers who are overtired or have used any alcohol or medications that make them sleepy.

Precautions also include using a firm mattress, keeping the baby away from pillows, and ensuring the baby cannot fall between the mattress and the wall or headboard. It is important to use a guardrail on the baby side of the adult bed or a "sidecar" baby bed that attaches to the adult bed so the baby does not fall. Be sure that the fabric liner is securely attached or not used at all to prevent the infant from becoming trapped between the edge of the mattress and the side of the sleeper.

SAFE SLEEP RECOMMENDATIONS

It is important to lay an infant down on his or her back without any loose clothing or sheets, pillows, toys or stuffed animals, or blankets, as these could be suffocation risks. It is not recommended to place an infant down on his or her stomach where airways might be blocked. Instead of using blankets, use a sleep sack for all infants until they can roll over unassisted; this is typically for at least the first six months of an infant's life and many parents decide not to allow blankets in an infant's bed until his or her first birthday.

Over the years, the American Academy of Pediatrics (AAP) has revised its recommendations for how infants should be put to sleep. While the recommendations above are still given, the AAP now also recommends that infants stay in a parent's room on a separate sleeping surface, such as a bassinet or a crib, until they are at least six months old and preferably one year old. This is to lower the risk of sudden infant death syndrome (SIDS), or the unexplained and sudden death of a seemingly healthy infant before the age of one.

If using a crib, the US Consumer Product Safety Commission (CPSC) has issued guidelines for safe crib use. New furniture sold online or in stores is required to conform to these rules. However, beware of older cribs. Check current safety standards from the CPSC. Decline buying or receiving cribs that don't meet them. The rules, updated in 2010, included:

- The crib should have a firm mattress with no space between the mattress and the frame.
- Screws, brackets, and other hardware must be in place and properly installed with none missing, loose, or broken.
- The maximum space between crib slats is 2 ⅜ inches (6 cm). This space prevents a baby's body from falling through them. No slats should be missing or broken.
- Any corner posts must be no higher than 1/16 inches (1.6 millimeters) to prevent the child's clothing from catching on them.
- There should be no cutouts (holes) in the headboard or footboard where a baby's head could get trapped.

For mesh-sided cribs or playpens, the mesh should be smaller than ¼ inch (6.35 mm) in diameter. The mesh should have no tears, holes, or loose threads and should be securely attached to the top rail and floor of the item.

The top rail should be covered with no tears or holes. No staples should be loose, missing, or exposed.

FURNISHING THE NURSERY

With these items on hand, make a list of what you'll need after the baby is born. A new parent needs a sling or soft infant carrier to keep the baby close during the day. A swing, bouncy seat, or other item can keep the baby safe when not in a parent's arms.

Every baby sooner or later needs a humidifier. Humidifiers release water particles into the air, increasing the humidity of a room. This can help ease congestion, which is especially important for infants, who should not be given any cold medication. And before you know it, you'll want a stroller and a highchair. An audio and/or video baby monitor will help you check on a sleeping baby (or older playing child) from another room in the house. Even if a mother decides not to breastfeed, a breastfeeding pillow is useful and supports the infant while you're holding or feeding him or her.

CAR SEATS

Perhaps the most important piece of equipment babies need is a properly installed car seat. Most hospitals will ask to see the car seat before letting you take the baby home. If you borrow or buy a used car seat, be sure

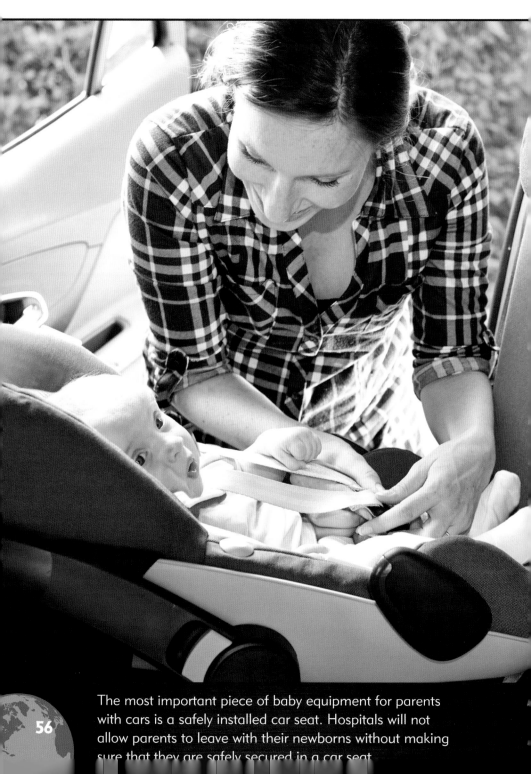

The most important piece of baby equipment for parents with cars is a safely installed car seat. Hospitals will not allow parents to leave with their newborns without making sure that they are safely secured in a car seat.

it has not previously been involved in a car accident—even a minor "fender bender." Also check with the manufacturer or online to be sure the model has not been involved in a safety recall. Most car seats expire after six to seven years, so be sure to check the expiration date sticker on the bottom of the car seat.

Choose a car seat based on the child's age, height, and weight. Some are made only for infants. Others convert as the child grows. According to the National Highway Traffic Safety Administration (NHTSA), children should stay in the same size seat as long as possible while they fit the height and weight requirements. And all children younger than thirteen years should ride in the back seat.

Carefully follow your vehicle owner's manual and the car seat manufacturer's installation instructions. Certified technicians are available to check your installation for free. Check the NHTSA website to find an inspection station near you.

CHAPTER 5

LABOR, BIRTH, AND RIGHT AFTER

Although fatigue is a common complaint with pregnancy, toward the end of the final trimester many women feel a burst of energy. They may feel restless to finish getting ready for the baby, such as cleaning up the house, doing loads of laundry, or finishing up the nursery. This is called nesting. It is an old wives' tale that labor is likely to start soon after the nesting urge begins. While it is possible that labor can shortly follow this burst of energy, it is still impossible to correctly determine when exactly labor will start on its own—and when expectant parents will be able to meet their new baby.

Labor is unpredictable and its onset cannot be reliably guessed or known. While this can be frustrating for expectant parents, it is exciting for them to think that they will soon be meeting their new baby.

Labor is the birth process. It begins with contractions of the uterus. Some describe them as cramping similar to the pulling and tightening sensation in the calf known as a charley horse. Others describe the feeling as pressure in the back or abdomen. The contractions get harder and closer together as birth nears. They cause the top part of the uterus to tighten and thicken while the bottom part stretches and relaxes. This helps the fetus move into the birth canal and out into the world.

Labor has four stages. For about 75 percent of first-time mothers, it lasts between fourteen and twenty-four hours, according to Tori Kropp, author of *The Joy of Pregnancy.*

THE FIRST STAGE

The first stage of labor takes the longest. It also is the easiest to manage. There are three phases to this stage:

- Early phase
- Active phase
- Transition phase

The early phase lasts about eight to twelve hours, and most laboring women stay home during this time. This phase thins the lower third of the uterus (called the cervix) and begins to widen it until it dilates to approximately 4 inches (10 cm). Contractions are irregular both in frequency and intensity. Laboring women should try not to focus too much on these early contractions. They are warming up the body for harder and more frequent contractions later.

THE 5-1-1 RULE

Many first-time mothers call their doctors or midwives upon feeling their first contractions, which can be too early and might lead to increased medical intervention. Most women can spend the early and active phases of labor at home and do not yet need to go to a hospital or birthing center. By staying at home during these early stages, laboring women can be more comfortable and more relaxed for the later stages of labor. A good rule of thumb about when to call your doctor or midwife is the 5-1-1 rule. Using a phone or a timer, time when each contraction begins and ends. Next, time how long there is between the end of one contraction and the beginning of another. Women should wait until they have contractions that are five minutes apart, which last for one minute each, and have been occurring for at least one hour before calling their doctor or midwife. It is not unusual for "false" contractions to begin weeks before true labor will start, but they will not form a predictable pattern or continue consistently. Even when real labor begins, it can take many hours before contractions are within five minutes of one another.

During this time, a woman in labor may feel aches in the back, legs, or lower abdomen. There may be diarrhea,mucus, or bloody vaginal discharge. This is called the "bloody show," and it's usually a reddish brown color.

If this phase begins at night, try to stay asleep. Even a short nap can be beneficial. Laboring women can also read or watch TV. During the day, stay upright or take a walk. (But it's not the time for a 5K run.) Stay active, but don't wear yourself out.

The active phase typically lasts from four to six hours. The cervix continues to widen, but it's not yet time for the baby to pass through it. Contractions are on a regular schedule about two or three minutes apart. They last about a minute and are intense enough to prevent talking or moving. This is a time to use breathing and relaxation techniques. Between contractions, a laboring woman can get a little rest and regroup or reposition.

The transition phase of early labor lasts only about one to three hours. This is the time the cervix widens to its maximum diameter (from about 2.8 inches to 3.9 inches, or 7 to 10 cm). This phase moves the action from stage one to stage two. Contractions last longer (about ninety seconds) and come one or two minutes apart. They are hardest to deal with. It is also the phase when some women who first chose unmedicated childbirth think they can't take any more intense or frequent contractions and ask for pain relief medication. For most women, however, stage two offers some relief from the transition phase.

THE SECOND STAGE

During the second stage, the baby begins to move through the birth canal. This is the pushing stage and is similar to but more intense than pushing out a bowel movement.

If a laboring woman has not had pain medication, her body will tell her when to push. The urge occurs with each contraction. She will bear down until the contraction ends. If she is medicated, the birth team will direct her when to push. The time between contractions often increases during this stage, which allows more time to rest

Timing contractions is a great way to know when it is time to

between them. Stage two lasts about one to three hours (depending somewhat on the size of the fetus). It ends with the baby's birth.

THE THIRD STAGE

Many women forget about the third stage of labor, or the delivery of the placenta. Soon after the baby's birth, the placenta detaches, and the uterus expels it. The placenta (also called the afterbirth) forms inside the uterus from the same cells that create the embryo. The placenta supplies nutrients and oxygen from the mother's blood. It also transfers waste products from the baby's blood to the mother's, where the mother's kidneys process it. The placenta helps start labor by producing necessary hormones.

Within about five minutes to thirty minutes after the baby's birth, it will again be time to push. This time, the process will be much easier than pushing out the baby. Once the placenta is delivered, the practitioner will press on the mother's abdomen or massage it until the uterus firms. A firm uterus prevents excessive bleeding from the detachment of the placenta.

The two hours after giving birth comprise an unofficial "stage four." This is known as the immediate postpartum period. If the mother plans to breastfeed, it starts now. During this time, caregivers will check to make sure the uterus is contracting. They'll also check for excessive bleeding.

NEWBORN HEALTH

An Apgar test measures five signs of a newborn's health. It helps medical personnel decide if the baby needs extra medical care. It tests the baby's heart rate, breathing, muscle tone, reflexes, and skin color. Health care providers perform the test twice. The first time is one minute after birth. The second time is four minutes later, when the baby is five minutes old. Apgar scores range from zero to ten. A score of seven or higher indicates a healthy baby. A baby who scores lower than that on the second screening needs additional medical attention and close monitoring.

Newborns need some additional tests, medicine, and procedures—some required by law. Eye drops or ointment often are applied to prevent blindness that can result from sexually transmitted infections of gonorrhea or chlamydia. Some parents at low risk for STDs prefer not to get these drops.

Newborns usually have low levels of vitamin K, a vitamin necessary for blood clotting. The American Academy of Pediatrics recommends a shot of vitamin K to prevent excessive bleeding. Another test is a metabolic screening. A small blood sample is taken from the baby's heel to test for phenylketonuria, galactosemia, hypothyroidism, and sickle cell disease. If the baby has any of these diseases, early treatment can prevent developmental disabilities, organ damage, blindness, or even death.

Newborns require certain screenings to make sure they are healthy enough to leave the hospital or birthing center. However, parents are given time to bond with their newborns immediately after birth before any interventions

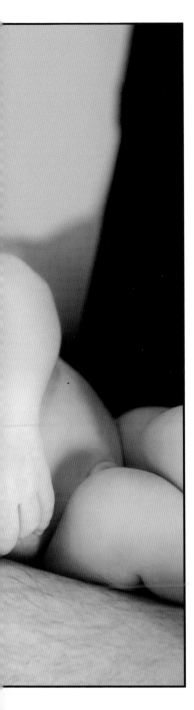

Newborns also get a hearing test. If a hearing disability is found early, the child can get a head start with treatment that can prevent speech and language delays. Finally, a vaccine that protects against hepatitis B virus (HPV) is recommended for newborns. The vaccine can prevent a lifelong infection, as well as liver damage and death. Full protection requires three shots during the first eighteen months of age. The American Academy of Pediatrics and the Centers for Disease Control recommend the first shot before leaving the hospital.

Medical personnel also check the baby's temperature, breathing, and heart rate and measure the baby's weight, length, and head circumference. They'll also bathe the baby and clean the area around the severed umbilical cord.

In the past babies were whisked away from their mothers so these interventions could be performed. However, many new mothers understand the need to bond with the baby as soon as possible after birth. The additional medical activities can be conducted an hour or so after birth. If you want to hold or nurse your baby right away, discuss the issue with your doctor or midwife during prenatal visits.

INDUCED LABOR

In some circumstances, practitioners may induce labor using medical procedures to get the birthing process going. One reason to consider induced labor is a pregnancy that goes beyond forty-two weeks, when a pregnancy is considered postterm. Some medical reasons to induce labor include:

- The fetus is growing so large vaginal delivery may become impossible if labor continues.
- The fetus is growing too slowly and doctors think the baby will be safer outside the uterus.
- The mother's health is threatened or a medical condition is getting worse.
- The amniotic fluid level is too low.

Some women request induction for convenience or other personal reasons. In the United States, elective induction of labor is one of the most commonly performed medical procedures. According to the Centers for Disease Control and Prevention, 23 percent of all of births are the result of induced labor with evidence suggesting that many of these are done for nonmedical reasons.

But choosing to induce labor is not without risk and should be considered carefully. According to the Mayo Clinic, induced labor often results in a C-section delivery, especially in women who have never given birth before and whose labor did not start on its own. Labor is a natural process that most often needs no medical intervention to begin. In most cases, it's best to let the baby arrive when he or she is ready.

CHAPTER 6

THE "FOURTH TRIMESTER"

The first three months of a baby's life are commonly known as the fourth trimester. This means that very young babies are completely helpless and dependent on a caregiver, and they take some time to adjust to their new world. They cannot feed themselves. They do not have control over their heads and cannot roll over or move to where food is. They cannot see well. They also cannot keep themselves safe, or warm, or dry.

So what do they do? They cry.

Crying is normal. In fact, it is a survival tool. It's the only way babies can communicate to get the care they need.

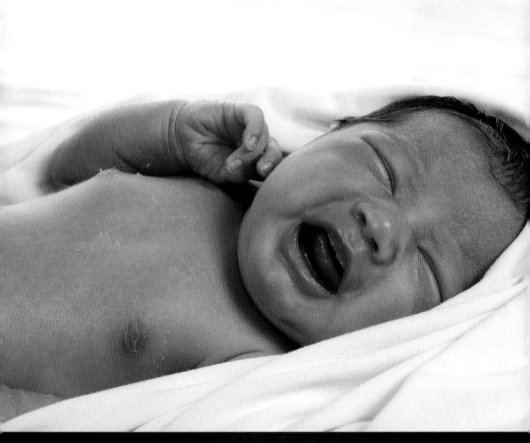

Newborns are completely dependent on their caregivers, which is why their first three months out of the womb are sometimes called the "fourth trimester."

A newborn's cry signals his or her entry into the world. Most babies cry the moment they breathe air for the first time. As they grow they cry for different reasons. Through trial and error, mothers can discover why babies cry in different situations. That helps them meet the child's needs.

What's important is to respond to any baby's cry quickly. Letting a very young baby "cry it out" can contribute to feelings of insecurity (although this technique can be used, within reason, for older babies). Sometimes a baby just needs to feel close contact with a parent or caregiver. Sometimes clothing is too tight or too scratchy. Or the crying may result from a number of other reasons. Stay calm and try to figure out what's wrong and what to do about it.

I'M HUNGRY

Hunger is a big reason babies cry. For the first month, most infants need nourishment about eight to twelve times a day. Their little stomachs can't hold enough milk to supply the calories they need less often than that. At the very least, a newborn needs to be fed about every four hours. So, hunger is your first best guess of why your baby is crying.

If a baby cries soon after a feeding, gas may be the problem. Prop the baby upright on your shoulder, and gently tap or rub the back. This may help bring up a burp that causes a tummy ache. Getting one burp may not be all that's needed. Continue tapping until the baby stops crying. You can also help a baby release gas by placing him or her on your lap in a sitting position. Support the head and chin and tap or rub the back. (Remember gas can escape through either end, so listen for both sounds. Or, wait for the baby's bowel movement, which may also relieve pain.) You can also soothe a crying baby by carrying him or her around the room with a rocking motion.

Babies cry when they are hungry. Newborns can cry a lot because their small stomachs can't hold much nourishment, and they need to be fed about eight to twelve times a day.

I'M IN PAIN

Teething can cause gum pain that makes a baby cry. Teething begins some time during a baby's first year. The timing is largely hereditary. As long as several weeks before the first tooth appears, the baby may gnaw on the fist or fingers. You may see a white spot on the gums.

The baby may be irritable and fussy, especially as the first tooth pushes against the gums. The pain may radiate to the jaw or ear. In response, the baby might rub the cheeks or pull on the ears. The baby may also have trouble sleeping.

A teething baby often drools, which may cause a rash on the chin. The excess saliva may also cause coughing or gagging. Babies put everything in their mouths, especially when teething. (So be sure to keep dangerous items out of reach.) The baby may also have a runny nose or a slight fever. (A high fever signals more worrisome illness. Call a doctor.)

Teething begins some time during a baby's first year. To

If you think your baby is crying because of teething, there are some steps you can take. Give the baby teething toys and rings. (Avoid toys with PVC or BPA, chemicals that can be poisonous to babies.) Look for toys meant to be kept in the refrigerator or freezer until used. The cool temperature soothes sore mouths. You can also freeze a clean, wet washcloth for the baby to suck on. Frozen melon, peaches, or carrots are cold treats that also relieve inflammation (cut small enough to prevent choking). You can also use a topical anesthetic gel or oral infant acetaminophen for pain.

I'M UNCOMFORTABLE

Babies sleep a lot. They often fall asleep on their own. But sometimes they cry or act fussy when they're tired. You may need to rock him or her to comfort and relax the baby. You can also walk around the room or push the baby in a stroller. Some

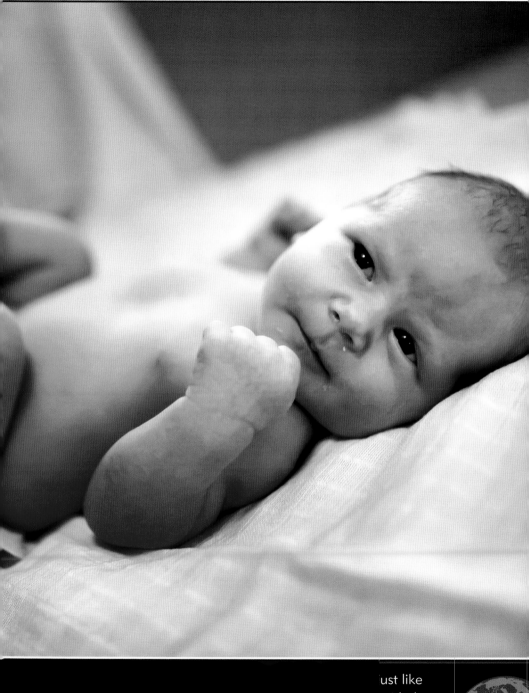

ust like
aided

parents resort to placing the baby in a car seat and going for a drive. Many babies are lulled to sleep by the motion of a motor vehicle.

Environmental factors can sometimes make a baby cry. In general, to be comfortable, most babies need the same temperature as the mother. If you need a sweater, put one on the baby, too. However, take care that the baby does not get overheated. Many caregivers rely on feeling the baby's hands or feet. But feeling the baby's tummy or neck is a more reliable measure of his or her temperature. Ann Peters, author of *Babycare: Everything You Need to Know,* suggests that the best room temperature for a sleeping baby is 64.4 degrees Fahrenheit (18 degrees Celsius).

A dirty diaper can cause discomfort when urine or feces comes in contact with the baby's skin. Be sure to keep the diaper area clean and immediately treat any diaper rash that develops with medication or over-the-counter cream or ointment.

COLIC

Colic is marked by continuous, inconsolable crying. It lasts as long as three hours and usually appears three or more days per week. It often begins at the same time of day or night.

Other signs include clenched fists and knees drawn up to the chest, which may indicate severe stomach pain. The baby may pass gas, again indicating stomach pain. The baby may appear stressed and have a red face. He or she may refuse to feed and have a hard time falling asleep or staying asleep.

According to Peters, about 20 percent of babies suffer from colic. It first appears between the ages of two to four weeks. It may last as long as three months—or even longer. The causes may vary from baby to baby. And doctors don't yet know what the causes are.

Some possibilities include sensitivity to the environment, discomfort, dairy intolerance, or other causes. A baby who is highly sensitive to the environment will also be sensitive to any changes in the environment. These include such factors as temperature, noise, amount of light, or even smell or taste. Discomfort may come from trapped gas. A bottle-fed baby may take in too much air along with the milk. Changing to a feeding system designed for babies with colic may ease the situation.

Dairy intolerance may be a problem, too. Some babies may react to proteins in dairy products. If the mother is breastfeeding, she may try eliminating dairy products in her diet to see if the colic improves. If bottle-feeding, the mother can switch to a hypoallergenic formula to see if that helps. Another suspect is the sugar found in milk. Some babies have trouble processing the sugar, called lactose. Babies getting formula with iron may become constipated—another potential source of stomachache. Consult a pediatrician to rule out these possibilities.

Dealing with a colicky baby can be stressful for caregivers, especially when it occurs at night and deprives them of sleep. Some ways to deal with the crying baby include using a pacifier and giving the baby a gentle massage or a warm, relaxing bath.

ILLNESS

A crying baby may be trying to indicate illness, especially if the crying is either weak or excessive. You may notice irritability or drowsiness. The baby may be reluctant to feed. But the first sign of illness often is a fever. The best place to check for fever is the back of the baby's neck. If it feels hotter than usual, use an under-arm digital thermometer or a digital ear thermometer. These are easy to use, but be sure to read directions carefully to get an accurate reading. According to the Mayo Clinic, if the baby is younger than three months, call a doctor for any fever. If the baby is three months or older, contact a doctor if the oral temperature is 102 °F (38.9 °C) or higher.

Also look for such other symptoms as failure to smile, fewer wet or dirty diapers than usual, rash, vomiting, or diarrhea. Call a doctor, urgent care center, or hospital emergency room as warranted.

10 GREAT QUESTIONS

TEN GREAT QUESTIONS TO ASK A HEALTH CARE PROVIDER

Your health care provider is there to answer all of the questions you might have as you go through this new experience. Here are some helpful questions you may want to ask him or her:

1. How should I change my diet to fit my baby's needs?

2. What kind of childbirth preparation do you recommend?

3. How much and what kind of exercise should I do while pregnant?

4. How much weight can I safely gain while pregnant?

5. What medicines can I safely take during pregnancy?

6. What are the risks of a vaginal birth compared to a cesarean section?

7. What should I know about breastfeeding, and is there a course on breastfeeding I can take prior to delivery?

8. What medical procedures will my child need immediately after birth?

9. What can I do to minimize the risk of sudden infant death syndrome (SIDS)?

10. How much should my baby be sleeping and eating in the first weeks following his or her birth?

CHAPTER 7

TAKING CARE OF BABY

It is not easy to take care of an infant. Infants require constant care and surveillance, which can often feel overwhelming for their primary caregiver. In addition to seeking help from friends and family, it is a good idea for parents to prepare before the birth to ease any anxiety they might have. Taking education classes and learning as much as they can about the care a baby needs will help them understand the role they will soon play. Many childbirth classes also include guidance for baby care, and soon-to-be-parents can ask a health care practitioner for information on new parent classes offered locally.

A great source of guidance and information for new parents is their baby's health care provider, who can answer any questions they might have.

FEEDING

Feeding the baby is the first priority. Experts agree that mother's milk is the best food for baby for the first year—or beyond. In fact, nursing for the first several days gives the infant the mother's immunities to illness through a substance called colostrum. Colostrum is the first breast milk produced. It contains antibodies that ward off disease.

Many women may struggle with breastfeeding. If not breastfeeding, commercial formula is available to bottle-feed the baby. Research has suggested that touching and the act of holding a baby during feeding may be what contributes most to the positive development and health benefits for the baby, whether or not the baby is breastfed. In both cases, milk is the most important part of an infant's diet. Babies should be fed when they're hungry (they'll let you know by acting fussy or crying). That may seem obvious. However, some new mothers try to put the baby on a feeding schedule. However, just like you, an infant is hungry at different times and ready for different amounts of food throughout the day. On-demand feeding is best for the baby and also ensures a breastfeeding mother's milk supply will replenish itself for the next feeding.

At some point around the six-month mark, with the advice of the baby's doctor, you can introduce solid foods. It's important to give only one new food at a time. This helps identify food allergies or sensitivities.

DIAPERING

Keeping the baby clean involves changing diapers and bathing the baby. Diaper changes are easy to do and usually not bad enough to gross you out. (If it is, take a deep breath and tough it out. You'll get used to it.)

INTRODUCING SOLIDS

Some parents are anxious to provide their children with additional nourishment to milk, such as rice cereal. They might believe that this helps a young infant sleep through the night. However, it is not recommended for babies under the age of at least four months and typically six months to have any nourishment other than breast milk or formula. If a baby is able to hold his or her head up and open his or her mouth when food is offered, this generally means he or she is ready for solid food.

Place the baby on a clean, wide surface and always keep one hand on her or him to prevent falls. Remove the dirty diaper. Use a damp washcloth or baby wipe to clean the entire bottom area. Wipe from front to back to help prevent urinary tract infections. An uncircumcised penis needs no special cleaning. Do *not* pull back the foreskin. Look for signs of diaper rash on the skin and use a medicated cream or ointment as needed. Put a new diaper on the baby. Dispose of the dirty diaper and wipes. Wash your hands with soap.

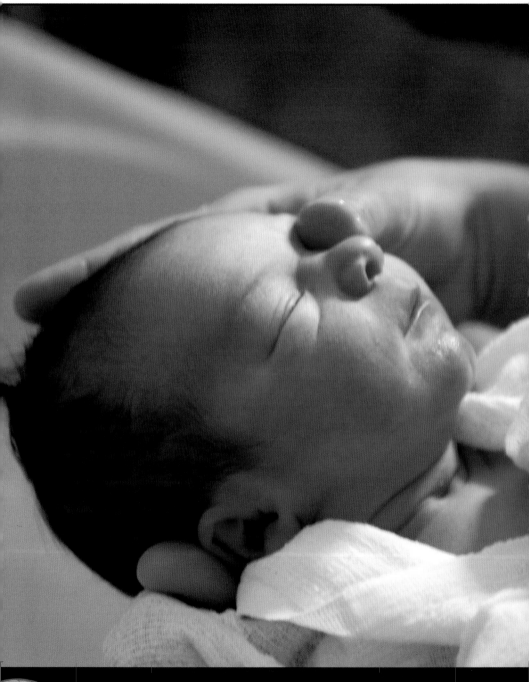

Baths no͏   ͏lso have a
relaxing ͏

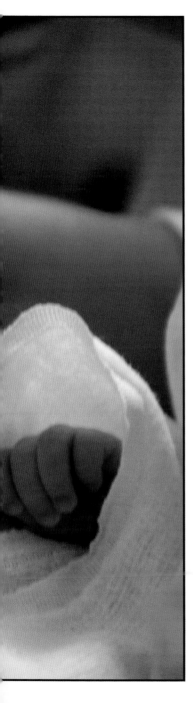

BATH TIME

Bathing the baby keeps him or her clean. It also has the same relaxing effect that it has on older children and adults. Until the umbilical cord stump falls off in a week to ten days, you'll need to give sponge baths. (The stump will fall off on its own, so keep it clean and dry until it does. To ensure that the area heals, resist the urge to pull on it, even if it's hanging on by a thread!) After that you can give baths in a sink, baby bathtub, or regular bathtub. (Be sure the tub is cleaned first if it is shared by other family members.)

Bathwater should be warm to the touch (test with your elbow or forearm). Just run a few inches of water in the bottom of the tub and place the baby in it. Use no-tears shampoo and soap designed for baby use. Try to keep the baby warm during the bath by pouring water over the skin from a plastic cup. As soon as you rinse, remove the baby from the water and wrap him or her in a warm towel. Diaper and dress the baby first. You can go back later to clean up the bath site. Always keep one hand in contact with the baby, and never leave him or her alone in a bath even for one single second. A baby can drown in a very small amount of water.

BEDTIME

When it's time for sleeping, place the infant on his or her back with the feet close to the foot of the crib. Be sure the crib sheet fits tightly. Remove any pillows, loose sheets, crib bumpers, stuffed animals, or dolls. Place the baby in a sleep sack or wrap him or her tightly in a swaddle. This is the safest position for the youngest children. As they grow and become able to roll over, they'll be able to reposition themselves for comfort without risking suffocation as long as the bed is otherwise clear.

BABY PROOFING

Your baby will not be mobile until typically at least six months, which means you will have some time to think about baby proofing

your house. However, there is no harm in getting a head start. While no house is 100 percent baby proof, you can take important actions to minimize the risk of injury and accident. Start with a smoke alarm on every level of your house. Check the batteries every time daylight savings time changes. Place lamps and other items at least three feet (one meter) from the crib. Tie up all electrical cords and keep the cords on blinds and shades out of reach. Install covers on all unused electrical sockets.

Prevent falls with baby gates at the tops of staircases. Use childproof locks on all cupboards and cabinets the baby can reach. Also store all medicines, cleaning supplies, alcohol, and toiletries high and locked up. And don't forget to secure garden chemicals and other items in the garage. Post phone numbers for poison control, doctors, and emergency contact individuals in an easy-to-see location or load them into your mobile phone.

Water hazards like swimming pools (even wading pools in the backyard) and ponds pose significant danger. Be sure to keep fences and gates locked. For home swimming pools, install an alarm that alerts you to anything (or anyone) falling into the water. You can teach your baby swim safety skills beginning as early as you can give him or her a bath. Check with the American Red Cross or your community pool for lessons.

BABYSITTING

Constant supervision is the best way to protect your child, especially outdoors. Never leave a child unattended at home or in public—especially in stores and parks. And never leave a child alone in a motor vehicle, even if you have to run into a store for just a minute.

Be cautious about who babysits for your child when you're away. Whether you're going to school or working, you may be able to leave the baby with a trusted relative or friend. Or, you might need the services of a nanny, or in-home or center-based day care provider. Many communities have resource and referral organizations that will help you find appropriate day care. Be sure to ask for background checks on all individuals who will have contact with your baby. Also ask whether the individual or staff is certified in first aid and CPR.

Once you start leaving your baby with someone, watch for signs that your child is being mistreated. If your child becomes withdrawn or has changes in eating or sleeping habits, he or she may be reacting to the situation. If the child suddenly gets upset when left with the caregiver, you may want to reconsider your caregiver. (But remember that some children experience anxiety when their mother leaves, no matter who the caregiver is.) Still, if you have any doubts, look for a different person to watch your child.

If someone is providing care in your own home, consider investing in a nanny cam, a hidden camera that lets you video record your nanny in action. You may also look for a system that lets you watch your baby live from your desk at work.

EASING THE TRANSITION FOR PETS

Dogs and cats can be sensitive to having a new person around—no matter how small. Cats usually have an

Dogs often have more difficulty adjusting to new babies in their homes than cats. To ease the transition, place an object with the baby's scent near your pet before introducing the baby.

easier time adjusting to the newcomer than dogs. Before introducing the baby, place a used blanket or piece of clothing with the baby's scent near a dog's bed or where a cat will find it. (If you're staying overnight in a hospital or birth center, ask a friend to do this for you before you come home.)

Remember to take the time to enjoy this brief period in your child's life. While taking care of a baby is a lot of work, it is also an incredibly special time in your lives.

For either species, greet the pet alone, outside the baby's presence. Bring the baby in and let the animal sniff him or her. Look for opportunities to pet or play with your pet when the baby is sleeping. However, cats may want to cuddle up with a sleeping child, which could be a smothering risk. Keep the cat out of the baby's sleeping room, and certainly out of the crib. Dogs, on the other hand, are pack animals. They want to be with you and the baby. So don't tie the dog outside or close him or her off in a separate room. The dog will come to protect the baby the same way he or she guards you.

ENJOY YOUR NEW BABY

Babies are not all work all the time, although it may occasionally seem so. Be sure to take the time to enjoy your infant. Cuddle the baby, or just hold him or her. The most important thing you can do is love your baby. The rest will come with time and practice.

ANEMIA A low number of red blood cells that causes weakness, fatigue, pale skin, or shortness of breath.

BIRTH PLAN A list of your preferences for what happens during and after the labor and birth experience.

CERVIX The lower third of the uterus.

COLIC Continuous, inconsolable crying that lasts for hours and usually occurs about the same time of day or night three or more times per week.

COLOSTRUM The first breast milk produced around the time of birth. It contains antibodies that ward off disease.

CONTRACTIONS Periodic tightening and relaxing of the uterus.

DAIRY INTOLERANCE A reaction to proteins in dairy products.

DOULA A nonmedical person trained in providing physical and emotional support during pregnancy, labor, birth, and the postpartum period.

EMBRYO A developing human from the time cells of a zygote start dividing until about eight weeks of growth.

FETUS A developing human between eight weeks of gestation and birth.

GESTATION The amount of time a baby grows in

the uterus.

HUMAN CHORIONIC GONADOTROPIN (HCG)
The pregnancy hormone that pregnancy tests
react to.

INDUCED LABOR Labor started with the use of
drugs or medical procedures.

LABOR The birthing process.

LACTOSE The carbohydrate (sugar) found
in milk.

OVULATION The release of an egg from the
ovary, which occurs monthly.

PLACENTA The organ that connects a fetus to the
wall of the uterus.

UMBILICAL CORD The cord that connects the
placenta to the developing embryo or fetus.

UTERUS A hollow, pear-shaped organ in a
woman's lower abdomen.

ZYGOTE A fertilized egg.

American Pregnancy Association (APA)
  1425 Greenway Drive
  Irving, Texas 75038
(972) 550-0140
Email: Questions@AmericanPregnancy.org
Website: www.americanpregnancy.org
Facebook: @AmericanPregnancyAssc
Twitter: @APAPregnancy
The American Pregnancy Association (APA)
  promotes reproductive and pregnancy
  wellness. It offers a toll-fee help line, website,
  and other forms of education, research,
  advocacy, and community awareness.

Canadian Association of Family Resource
  Programs (FRP Canada)
  707 - 331 Cooper Street
  Ottawa, ON K2P 0G5
  Canada
(866) 637-7226
Email: info@frp.ca
Website: www.frb.ca
Facebook: @FRPCanada
Twitter: @FRPCanada
FRP is a Canadian association of programs that
  provide resources through leadership and
  consultation for those who care for children
  and support families.

Canadian Association of Pregnancy Support
    Services (CAPSS)
    304 - 4820 Gaetz Avenue
    Red Deer, AB T4N 4A4
    Canada
(866) 845-2151
Website: www.capss.com
Facebook: @Canadian Association of Pregnancy
    Support Services
CAPSS is a nonpolitical, Christian charity
    that equips pregnancy support service
    centers across Canada. These centers
    provide practical, material, emotional, and
    spiritual help for families and women with
    distressing pregnancies.

International Childbirth Education Association
    (ICEA)
    110 Horizon Drive, Suite 210
    Raleigh, NC 27607
    (800) 624-4934
Website: www.icea.org
Email: info@icea.org
Facebook: @ICEApage
Twitter: @ICEA_org
The International Childbirth Education
    Association (ICEA) is a nonprofit, professional
    organization. It provides training, educational

resources, and professional certification
programs for educators and health care
providers who help women make decisions
based on knowledge of alternatives in
maternity and newborn care.

National Campaign to Prevent Teen and
Unplanned Pregnancy
1776 Massachusetts Avenue NW, Suite 200
Washington, DC 20036
(202) 478-8500
Website: www.thenationalcampaign.org
Facebook: @TheNationalCampaign
Twitter: @TheNC
The National Campaign to Prevent Teen
and Unplanned Pregnancy is a private,
nonpartisan organization that seeks to prevent
unplanned pregnancy, especially among
unmarried young adults.

Parents Without Partners (PWP)
1100-H Brandywine Boulevard
Zanesville, OH 43701
(800) 637-7974
Email: Intl.HQ@ParentsWithoutPartners.org
Website: www.parentswithoutpartners.org
Facebook: @parentswithoutpartnersinternational
Parents Without Partners is an international,

nonprofit membership organization for single parents and their children. It provides educational and social activities that offer support, friendship, and exchange of parenting techniques. It also offers activities for children in single-parent families.

Planned Parenthood Federation of America (PPFA)
123 William Street
New York, NY 10038
(212) 541-7800
Website: www.plannedparenthood.org
Facebook: @PlannedParenthood
Twitter: @PPFA
Planned Parenthood is a sexual and reproductive health care provider. It provides sex education and advocates for the reproductive health and rights movement.

Women, Infants, and Children (WIC)
US Department of Agriculture
1400 Independence Avenue SW
Washington, DC 20250
(202) 720-2791
Email: wichq-web@vns.usda.gov
Website: www.fns.usda.gov/wic
Facebook: @USDA

Twitter: @USDANutrition

WIC is a government program administered by the US Department of Agriculture through state agencies. It provides food, information on healthy eating, and referrals to health care for women, infants, and children up to age five who are nutritionally at risk.

WEBSITES

Due to the changing nature of internet links, Rosen Publishing has developed an online list of websites related to the subject of this book. This site is updated regularly. Please use this link to access the list:

http://www.rosenlinks.com/WITW/Teen

Brott, Armin A., and Jennifer Ash. *The Expectant Father: The Ultimate Guide For Dads-To-Be.* New York, NY: Abbeville Press, 2015.

Deering, Kathryn. *A Little Book of Tweets for Moms.* Uhrichsville, OH: Barbour Publishing, 2012.

Doherty, Emily. *Funny Little Pregnancy Things: The Good, the Bad, and the Just Plain Gross Things About Pregnancy That Other Books Aren't Going to Tell You.* Tempe, AZ: SparkPress, 2016.

Erdmans, Mary Patrice, and Timothy Black. *On Becoming a Teen Mom: Life Before Pregnancy.* Oakland, CA: University of California Press, 2015.

Ford, Amy. *A Bump in Life: True Stories of Hope and Courage During An Unplanned Pregnancy.* Nashville, TN: B&H Books, 2013.

Goyer, Tricia. *Teen Mom: You're Stronger Than You Think.* Grand Rapids, MI: Zondervan, 2015.

McGill, Elizabeth. *Pregnancy Information for Teens: Health Tips About Teen Pregnancy and Teen Parenting.* Detroit, MI: Omnigraphics, 2012.

Pipkin, Bonnie. *Aftercare Instructions: A Novel.* New York, NY: Flatiron Books, 2017.

Riley, Laura. *You and Your Baby Pregnancy: The Ultimate Week-by-Week Pregnancy Guide.* Hoboken, NJ: John Wiley & Sons Inc., 2012.

Rodriguez, Gaby, and Jenna Glatzer. *The Pregnancy Project: A Memoir.* New York, NY: Simon & Schuster Books for Young Readers, 2013.

Space, Darell. *Pregnancy: For First Time Moms, What They Don't Tell You.* CreateSpace, 2014.

Spock, Benjamin. *Dr. Spock's Baby and Child Care.* New York, NY: Gallery Books, 2012.

Thomas, Paul, and Jennifer Margulis. *The Vaccine-Friendly Plan: Dr. Paul's Safe and Effective Approach to Immunity and Health— From Pregnancy Through Your Child's Teen Years.* New York, NY: Ballantine Books, 2016.

Alphonse, Lylah M. "Is Crying it Out Dangerous for Kids?" Parenting, December 14, 2011. http://us.lifestyles.qa1p.global.media.yahoo .com/parenting/crying-dangerous-kids-one -expert-says-222400379.html.

Bohn, Yvonne, Allison Hill, and Alane Park. *The Mommy Docs' Ultimate Guide to Pregnancy and Birth*. Cambridge, MA: Da Capo Press, 2011.

Contracept.com. "Understanding Your Risks." Contracept, 2011. http://www.contracept.org /risks.php.

CoolNurse. "Teen Pregnancy." Livestrong, August 11, 2011. http://www.livestrong.com /article/12457-teen-pregnancy.

Dahl, Gordon B. "Early Teen Marriage and Future Poverty." *Demography*, Vol. 47, No. 3, August, 2010, pp. 689-718.

Kropp, Tori. *The Joy of Pregnancy*. Boston, MA: The Harvard Common Press, 2008.

Landau, Erika, and Abigail Brenner. *The Essential Guide to Baby's First Year*. New York, NY: Alpha Books, 2011.

Lane, Brenda J., and Ilana T. Kirsch. *Knack Pregnancy Guide: An Illustrated Handbook for Every Trimester*. Guilford, CT: Knack, 2009.

Leeds, Regina. *One Year to an Organized Life with Baby*. Cambridge, MA: Da Capo Press, 2011.

Mayo Clinic Staff. "Sick Baby? When To Seek
    Medical Attention." Mayo Clinic, February 2,
    2011. http://www.mayoclinic.com/health
    /healthy-baby/PR00022.
McKenna, James J. "Cosleeping and Biological
    Imperatives: Why Human Babies Do
    Not and Should Not Sleep Alone."
    Neuroanthropology, December 21, 2008.
    https://neuroanthropology.net/2008/12/21
    /cosleeping-and-biological-imperatives-why
    -human-babies-do-not-and-should-not
    -sleep-alone.
Peters, Ann. *Babycare: Everything You Need To
    Know.* New York, NY: Dorling Kindersley
    Limited, 2011.
Ricciotti, Hope, and Vincent Connelly. *I'm
    Pregnant! Now What Do I Eat?* New York, NY:
    Dorling Kindersley Limited, 2007.
Stein, Rob. "Rise in Teenage Pregnancy
    Rate Spurs New Debate on Arresting It."
    Washington Post, January 26, 2010. http://
    www.washingtonpost.com/wp-dyn/content
    /article/2010/01/25/AR2010012503957.html.
Sutter Health. "Amniotic Fluid/Bag of Water."
    Retrieved March 3, 2017. http://www.babies
    .sutterhealth.org/laboranddelivery/ld_am
    -flu.html.

Sutton, Amy L. *Pregnancy and Birth Sourcebook.*
Detroit, MI: Omnigraphics, 2009.
US Consumer Product Safety Commission.
"Learn How to Put Your Baby to Sleep Safely."
Retrieved March 3, 2017. https://www.cpsc
.gov/Safety-Education/Safety-Education
-Centers/cribs.
WebMD Editors. "Pregnancy and Conception."
WebMD, 2007. http://www.webmd.com/baby
/guide/understanding-conception#1.

INDEX

A

abstinence, 12
alcohol, 37, 52
anemia, 45
Apgar test, 65
Assisting Young Mothers
    Program, 18

B

baby clothes, 50
baby monitor, 55
baby proofing, 88, 90
babysitters, screening and
    monitoring, 91–92
bathing, 80, 84, 87–88
birth coach, 25, 34
birth hypnosis, 25
Birthing from Within,
    24, 25
birth plan, 29–31
Birth Works, 24
bloody show, 62
bonding, 25, 52, 68
bottle-feeding, 50, 79, 84
Bradley Method, 24, 25
breastfeeding, 19, 25, 33,
    37, 50, 52, 55, 64, 79,
    81, 84
    and immunity to
    illness, 83

and ovulation, 47
breastfeeding pillow, 55
breast pump, 50

C

caffeine, 37, 47
calorie consumption,
    extra for baby, 47
car seats, 55, 57
cervix, 43, 60, 62
cesarean section
    (C-section), 27, 29,
    33, 69, 81
checkups, 35
childbirth classes,
    24–25, 82
colic, 78–80
colostrum, 83
complications, 24, 45–46
condoms, 12
contraception, 8, 10–12, 28
contractions, 43, 59, 60,
    61, 62, 63
cosleeping, 52
counselors, 17
cravings, 40
cribs, safety guidelines
    for, 54
crying, reasons for,
    70–72, 74, 76, 78–80

ABOUT THE AUTHORS

Lena Koya is a writer and scholar based in Long Island, New York. While working on this book, she was awaiting the birth of her second boy. She enjoys spending time with her family, including her son Theo and her husband, Fadi.

Mary-Lane Kamberg is a professional writer and speaker in Olathe, Kansas. One of her two daughters is a certified Bradley Method childbirth instructor.

PHOTO CREDITS